Miss Bunny

Size: 13½ inches W x 42¾ inches H
(34.3cm x 108.6cm)
Skill Level: Intermediate

Materials

❏ Clear 7-count stiff plastic canvas:
  2 (13½ x 22½-inch) sheets
  1 (12 x 18-inch) sheet
❏ Medium weight yarn as listed in color key
❏ ¼-inch-wide (6.5mm) satin ribbon:
  1 yard (1m) each pink, blue, green, yellow,
  orange, purple
❏ Small amount of fiberfill
❏ ½ x 1-inch (11.4cm x 2.5cm) piece
  foam-core board
❏ Yardstick
❏ Standard-size brick
❏ #16 tapestry needle
❏ Hot-glue gun

Stitching Step by Step

Cutting

1 *Bunny:* Cut one feet piece according to graph. Cut two bodies and two heads, joining graphs for top and bottom portions before cutting each as one piece. Carefully trim gray shaded areas around paws on body pieces.

2 *Braces and joining strips:* Cut one piece 76 holes x 6 holes for body brace A; one piece 78 holes x 6 holes for body brace B; one piece 80 holes x 6 holes for body brace C; two pieces 16 holes x 10 holes for head braces; one piece 82 holes x 6 holes for feet/body joining strip; and one piece 65 holes x 6 holes for body/head joining strip.

3 *Base:* Cut one base top according to graph. Also cut two pieces 53 holes x 26 holes for base front and back, and cut two pieces 17 holes x 26 holes for base ends.

4 *Flowers:* Cut two according to graph.

5 *Eggs:* Cut 12 egg shapes in all according to graphs— two each of *A, S, T* and *R,* and four of *E.*

Bunny & Base

1 *Base:* Stitch base top according to graph; Overcast edges between red arrows. Using same pattern, stitch both ends and *one* of the front/back pieces. The unstitched piece will be the base front (next to Miss Bunny's reverse side).

2 Work background stitches on feet piece according to graph, *leaving the last three rows along the top edge unstitched for now where indicated by green shading.*

3 Using tan yarn, Whipstitch base ends to short edges of unstitched base front. Center base front on reverse side of stitched feet with bottom edges even; holding base front in place, work white Backstitches down center of white dress hem and dark brown Backstitches on feet according to graph, working through both layers as needed.

4 Using tan yarn and referring to base assembly diagram throughout, Whipstitch stitched base back to base ends. Whipstitch base top to base ends and back so that Overcast edge is adjacent to bunny feet.

5 *Body:* Holding bunny body pieces together, stitch according to graph, working through both layers, and *leaving three rows along top and bottom edges unstitched for now as indicated by green shading.* When stitching apron, work dark green Straight Stitches first, then upright Cross Stitches.

6 Sandwich top edge of feet/body joining strip between the unstitched rows at the bottom of the body pieces; align bottom half of strip behind unstitched rows at top of feet. Stitch through all layers to join feet to body.

7 *Head:* Stitch rose inner ear on *one* head according to graph. Trim foam-core board to fit behind stitched area. Hold second head behind the first, and working through both layers, stitch head according to graph, inserting foam core board into ear behind rose stitched center (trim end of foam core strip at an angle as needed to fit in space); *leave bottom three rows of head unstitched for now as indicated by green shading.*

8 Center and sandwich edges of body/head joining strip between the unstitched rows at the top of the body and the bottom of the head pieces. Stitch through all layers to join body to head.

9 Overcast cutout edges around paws using tan, light green and dark green according to body graph.

10 *Work embroidery stitches:* Using rose, Backstitch between nose and mouth. Using dark brown, Backstitch ear. Using dark pink, Straight Stitch buttons. Using dark green, Backstitch and Straight Stitch arms and apron. Referring to stitch diagram, work Unclipped Turkey Loop Stitches around neckline (dark pink, light green and dark green) and hem (white and light green).

11 Position body brace strips A–C across reverse side of bunny in rows indicated by blue arrows on body graphs. Overcast bunny edges according to graph, Whipstitching ends of body braces as you stitch.

12 Center head braces on reverse side of bunny head in rows indicated by blue arrows on head graphs. Whipstitch short ends of brace to head, working under stitches on reverse side of bunny only.

Flowers

1 Stitch one flower according to graph; Overcast edges. Stitch the second flower substituting light blue for light purple and dark blue for dark purple.

2 Using light yellow and referring to the stitch diagram, work three Clipped Turkey Loop Stitches in the center of each flower; frizz ends with a needle.

3 Hot-glue flowers to hat as shown.

Eggs

1 Stitch all eggs according to graphs, substituting dark purple for dark pink and light purple for light pink on two of the *E* eggs.

2 Whipstitch eggs together in matching pairs using adjacent colors, stuffing each egg with fiberfill to give it dimension.

3 Thread matching ribbon through top of each egg. Tie ribbons for *E, A* and *S* eggs in one cluster, tying ends in a decorative bow; repeat with remaining eggs. Tie, hot-glue or stitch ribbons of *EAS* eggs to bunny's left hand and *TER* eggs to right hand.

Final Assembly

Insert brick into base through open bottom. Slide yardstick down back of bunny, through all brace strips and into base.

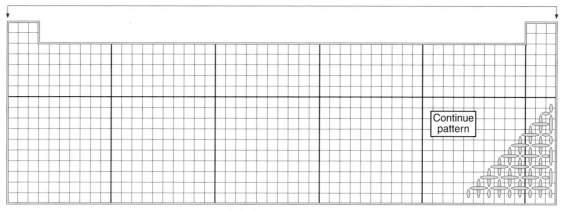

Miss Bunny Base Top
53 holes x 17 holes
Cut 1

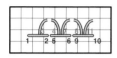

Clipped Turkey Loop

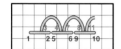

Unclipped Turkey Loop

Continue pattern

Miss Bunny Flower
14 holes x 14 holes
Cut 2
Stitch 1 as graphed; stitch 1 substituting light
blue for light purple and dark blue for dark purple

COLOR KEY

Yards	Medium Weight Yarn
150 (137.2m)	☐ Tan
120 (109.8m)	☐ Light green
100 (91.5m)	■ Dark pink
50 (45.8m)	■ Dark green
50 (45.8m)	☐ White
25 (22.9m)	■ Rose
10 (9.2m)	■ Dark blue
10 (9.2m)	☐ Light blue
10 (9.2m)	☐ Light orange
10 (9.2m)	☐ Light pink
10 (9.2m)	☐ Light purple
10 (9.2m)	☐ Light yellow
6 (5.5m)	■ Dark purple
5 (4.6m)	■ Dark brown
5 (4.6m)	■ Dark orange
4 (3.7m)	☐ Dark yellow
3 (2.8m)	■ Brown
1 (1m)	■ Navy blue
✎	Dark brown Backstitch
✎	Rose Backstitch
✎	White Backstitch
✎	Dark blue Straight Stitch
✎	Dark green Backstitch and Straight Stitch
✎	Dark pink Straight Stitch
●	Dark green Unclipped Turkey Loop Stitch
○	Light green Unclipped Turkey Loop Stitch
●	Dark pink Unclipped Turkey Loop Stitch
○	White Unclipped Turkey Loop Stitch
○	Light yellow Unclipped Turkey Loop Stitch

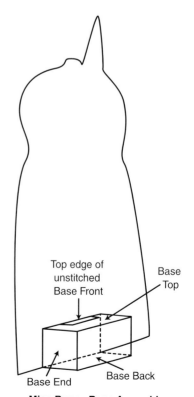

Top edge of
unstitched
Base Front

Base
Top

Base End

Base Back

Miss Bunny Base Assembly

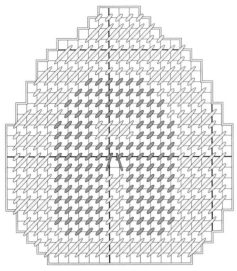

Miss Bunny "A" Egg
22 holes x 24 holes
Cut 2

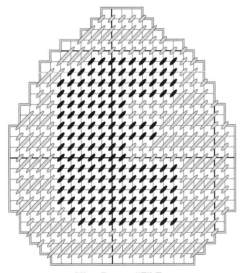

Miss Bunny "E" Egg
22 holes x 24 holes
Cut 4
Stitch 2 as graphed; stitch 2 substituting dark
purple for dark pink and light purple for light pink

COLOR KEY	
Yards	**Medium Weight Yarn**
150 (137.2m)	☐ Tan
120 (109.8m)	☐ Light green
100 (91.5m)	■ Dark pink
50 (45.8m)	■ Dark green
50 (45.8m)	☐ White
25 (22.9m)	■ Rose
10 (9.2m)	■ Dark blue
10 (9.2m)	☐ Light blue
10 (9.2m)	☐ Light orange
10 (9.2m)	☐ Light pink
10 (9.2m)	■ Light purple
10 (9.2m)	☐ Light yellow
6 (5.5m)	■ Dark purple
5 (4.6m)	■ Dark brown
5 (4.6m)	■ Dark orange
4 (3.7m)	☐ Dark yellow
3 (2.8m)	■ Brown
1 (1m)	■ Navy blue
	╱ Dark brown Backstitch
	╱ Rose Backstitch
	╱ White Backstitch
	╱ Dark blue Straight Stitch
	╱ Dark green Backstitch and Straight Stitch
	╱ Dark pink Straight Stitch
	● Dark green Unclipped Turkey Loop Stitch
	○ Light green Unclipped Turkey Loop Stitch
	● Dark pink Unclipped Turkey Loop Stitch
	○ White Unclipped Turkey Loop Stitch
	○ Light yellow Unclipped Turkey Loop Stitch

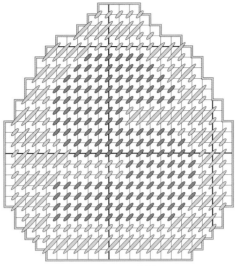

Miss Bunny "S" Egg
22 holes x 24 holes
Cut 2

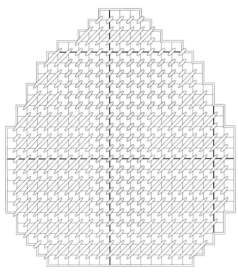

Miss Bunny "T" Egg
22 holes x 24 holes
Cut 2

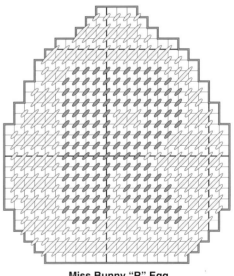

Miss Bunny "R" Egg
22 holes x 24 holes
Cut 2

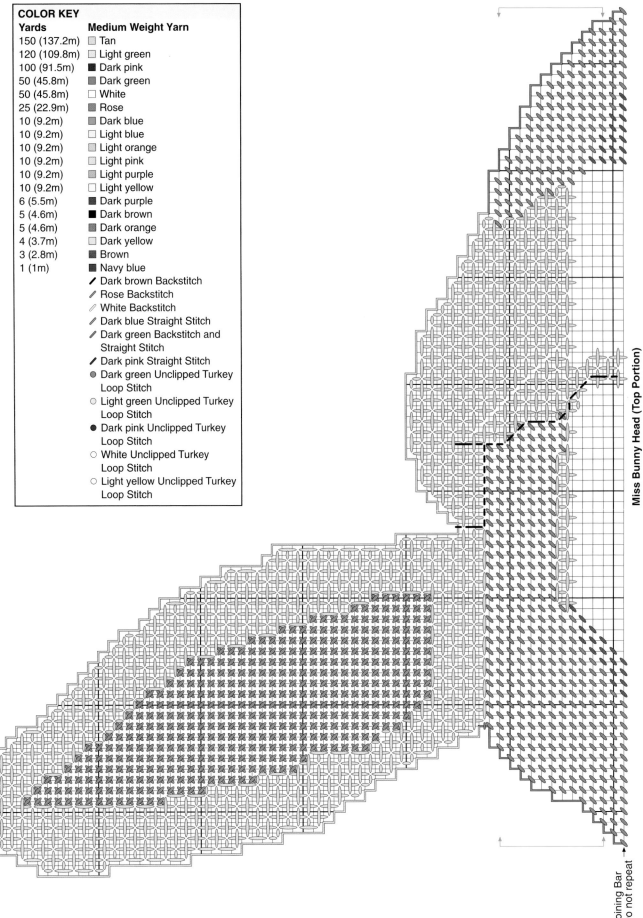

COLOR KEY

Yards	Medium Weight Yarn
150 (137.2m)	Tan
120 (109.8m)	Light green
100 (91.5m)	Dark pink
50 (45.8m)	Dark green
50 (45.8m)	White
25 (22.9m)	Rose
10 (9.2m)	Dark blue
10 (9.2m)	Light blue
10 (9.2m)	Light orange
10 (9.2m)	Light pink
10 (9.2m)	Light purple
10 (9.2m)	Light yellow
6 (5.5m)	Dark purple
5 (4.6m)	Dark brown
5 (4.6m)	Dark orange
4 (3.7m)	Dark yellow
3 (2.8m)	Brown
1 (1m)	Navy blue
	Dark brown Backstitch
	Rose Backstitch
	White Backstitch
	Dark blue Straight Stitch
	Dark green Backstitch and Straight Stitch
	Dark pink Straight Stitch
	Dark green Unclipped Turkey Loop Stitch
	Light green Unclipped Turkey Loop Stitch
	Dark pink Unclipped Turkey Loop Stitch
	White Unclipped Turkey Loop Stitch
	Light yellow Unclipped Turkey Loop Stitch

Miss Bunny Head (Top Portion)
87 holes x 134 holes
Cut 2, joining with graph for bottom portion before cutting each as 1 piece

Joining Bar
Do not repeat

Continue pattern

Miss Bunny Head (Bottom Portion)
87 holes x 134 holes
Cut 2, joining with graph for top portion before cutting each as 1 piece

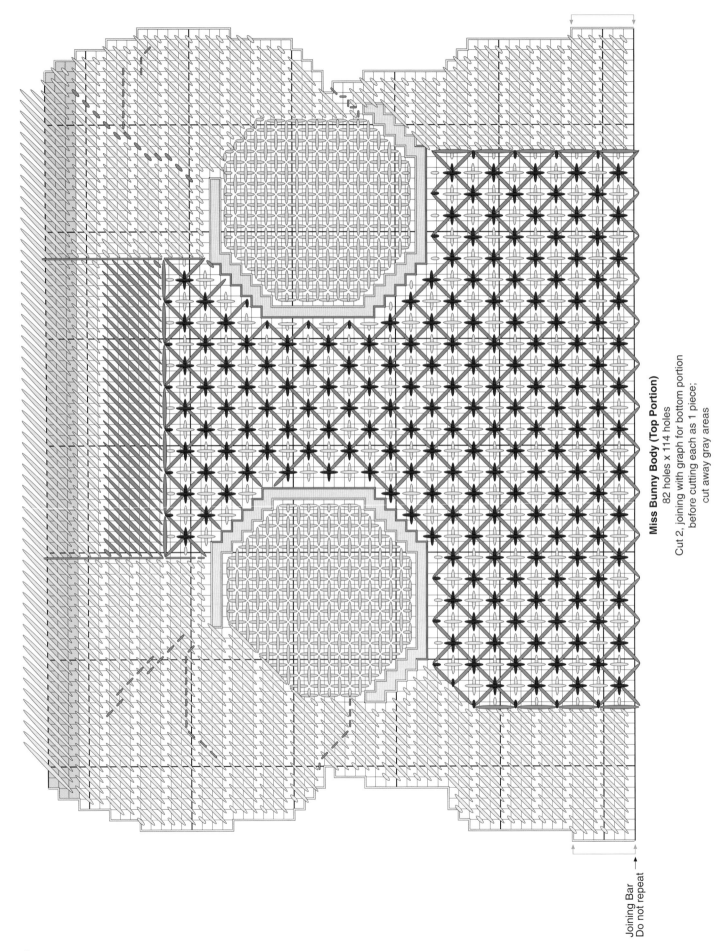

Miss Bunny Body (Top Portion)
82 holes x 114 holes
Cut 2, joining with graph for bottom portion
before cutting each as 1 piece;
cut away gray areas

Joining Bar
Do not repeat

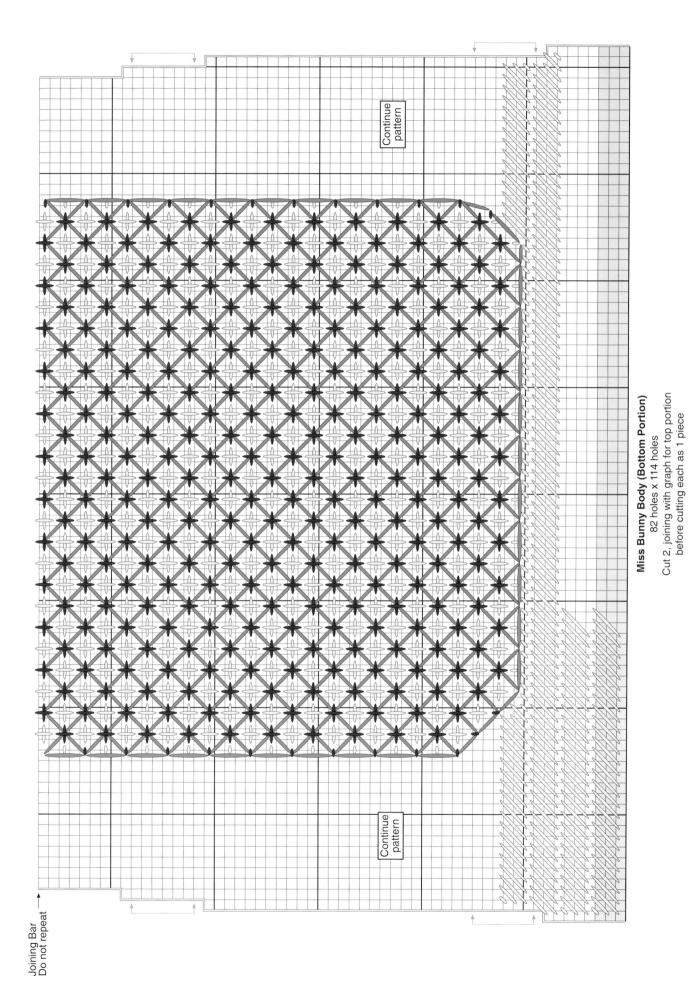

Miss Bunny Body (Bottom Portion)
82 holes x 114 holes
Cut 2, joining with graph for top portion
before cutting each as 1 piece

Continue pattern

Continue pattern

Joining Bar
Do not repeat

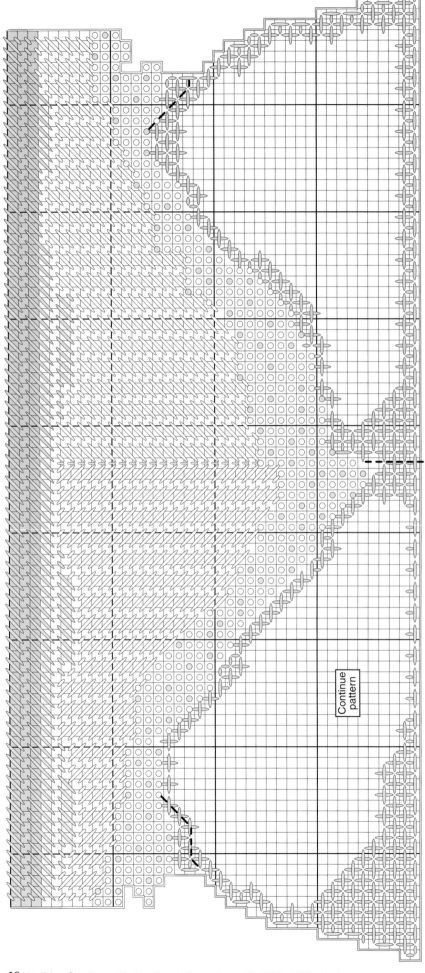

Miss Bunny Feet
91 holes x 40 holes
Cut 1

Continue pattern

COLOR KEY

Yards	Medium Weight Yarn
150 (137.2m)	Tan
120 (109.8m)	Light green
100 (91.5m)	Dark pink
50 (45.8m)	Dark green
50 (45.8m)	White
25 (22.9m)	Rose
10 (9.2m)	Dark blue
10 (9.2m)	Light blue
10 (9.2m)	Light orange
10 (9.2m)	Light pink
10 (9.2m)	Light purple
10 (9.2m)	Light yellow
6 (5.5m)	Dark purple
5 (4.6m)	Dark brown
5 (4.6m)	Dark orange
4 (3.7m)	Dark yellow
3 (2.8m)	Brown
1 (1m)	Navy blue
╱	Dark brown Backstitch
╱	Rose Backstitch
╱	White Backstitch
╱	Dark blue Straight Stitch
╱	Dark green Backstitch and Straight Stitch
╱	Dark pink Straight Stitch
●	Dark green Unclipped Turkey Loop Stitch
○	Light green Unclipped Turkey Loop Stitch
●	Dark pink Unclipped Turkey Loop Stitch
○	White Unclipped Turkey Loop Stitch
○	Light yellow Unclipped Turkey Loop Stitch

Firecracker

Size: 21½ inches W x 31½ inches H
(54.6cm x 80cm)
Skill Level: Intermediate

Materials

❑ Clear 7-count stiff plastic canvas:
   2 (13½ x 22½-inch) sheets
   2 (12 x 18-inch) sheets
❑ Medium weight yarn as listed in color key
❑ Uniek Needloft metallic craft cord as listed
   in color key
❑ Kreinik Heavy (#32) Braid as listed in color key
❑ 4-inch (10.2cm) strip hook-and-loop fastening tape
❑ 6½ x 28½-inch (16.5cm x 72.4cm) piece
   foam-core board
❑ Standard-size brick
❑ #16 tapestry needle
❑ Hot-glue gun

Stitching Step by Step

Cutting

1 *Firecracker:* Cut two heads, two bodies, two right arms and two left arms according to graphs, cutting gray shaded areas from only one of each arm.

2 *Braces:* Cut one piece 53 holes x 6 holes and two pieces 53 holes x 9 holes; they will remain unstitched.

3 *Base:* Cut one base top, one base back and two base ends according to graphs.

4 *Explosion:* Cut one according to graph.

Firecracker & Base

1 *Head:* Holding pieces together, stitch head according to graph, working through both layers.

2 Referring to stitch diagram (page 17), work Diagonal Rhodes Stitches on head using white iridescent craft cord; work crisscrossed Straight Stitches using craft cord and red heavy (#32) braid according to graph.

3 Overcast side and top edges according to graph; leave bottom edges unfinished for now.

4 *Body:* Holding body pieces together, stitch according to graph, working through both layers; fill ungraphed center with pattern of red and white blocks, and *leave green shaded areas in upper corners unstitched for now.*

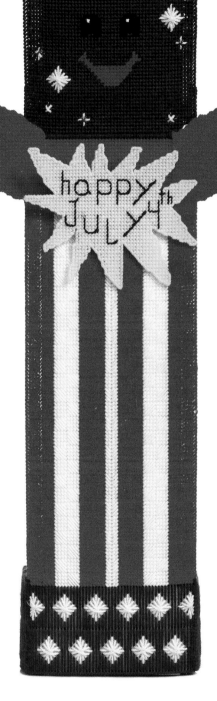

5 When background stitching is complete, work Diagonal Rhodes Stitches on blue area using white iridescent craft cord.

6 *Arms:* Using red yarn, Overcast the cutout openings in arms; these arms will be on front. Holding arms together in matching pairs, stitch according to graph, working through both layers and *leaving areas unstitched for now where indicated by green shading.*

7 Slide unstitched upper right corner of body between open edges of right arm, aligning unstitched areas; stitch through all layers, completing stitching on arm and Whipstitching overlapping edges of arm to body as you stitch. Repeat with left arm.

8 *Base:* Stitch base top, back and ends according to graphs. Overcast edges of top between red arrows.

9 Referring to base assembly diagram (page 17) and using royal blue yarn throughout, Whipstitch base ends to short edges of base back. Whipstitch top to base ends and back. Whipstitch remaining edges of base ends to edges of body with bottom edges even; Overcast bottom edges.

10 Position brace strips across reverse side of firecracker where indicated by blue arrows on body and head graphs. Overcast firecracker edges according to graph, Whipstitching ends of braces strips as you stitch.

Explosion

1 Fill in uncoded explosion with yellow Continental Stitches, Overcasting edges as you stitch.

2 When background stitching is complete, Backstitch lettering using brown yarn.

3 Center and hot-glue half of the hook-and-loop strip to body over seam between solid red and striped stitching; hot-glue remaining half to matching position on reverse side of explosion. Affix explosion to firecracker as shown.

Final Assembly

Insert brick into base through open bottom. Slide foam-core board down back of firecracker, through all brace strips and into base.

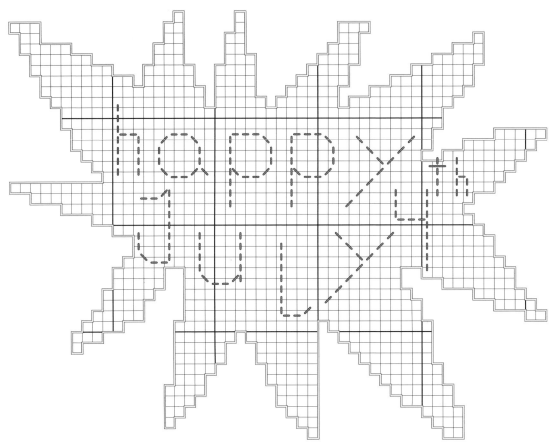

Firecracker Explosion
52 holes x 40 holes
Cut 1

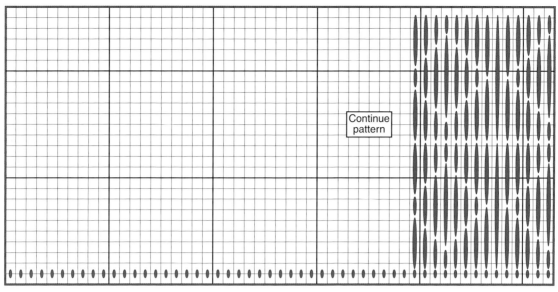

Firecracker Base Back
53 holes x 26 holes
Cut 1

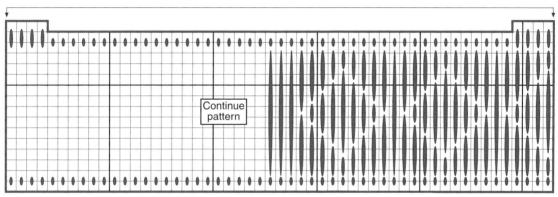

Firecracker Base Top
53 holes x 16 holes
Cut 1

COLOR KEY

Yards	Medium Weight Yarn
75 (68.6m)	■ Red
55 (50.3m)	■ Royal blue
50 (45.8m)	☐ White
5 (4.5m)	☐ Yellow
2 (1.9m)	☐ Medium blue
1 (1m)	■ Black
1 (1m)	■ Brown

Uncoded areas on Explosion are yellow Continental Stitches

⟋ Brown Backstitch

Iridescent Craft Cord

8 (7.4m)	⟋ White #55033 Straight Stitch and Diagonal Rhodes Stitch

Heavy (#32) Braid

3 (2.8m)	⟋ Red hi lustre #003HL Straight Stitch

Color numbers given are for Uniek Needloft iridescent craft cord and Kreinik Heavy (#32) Braid.

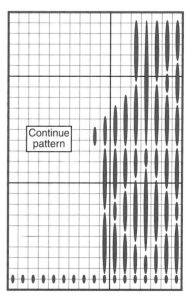

Firecracker Base End
17 holes x 26 holes
Cut 2

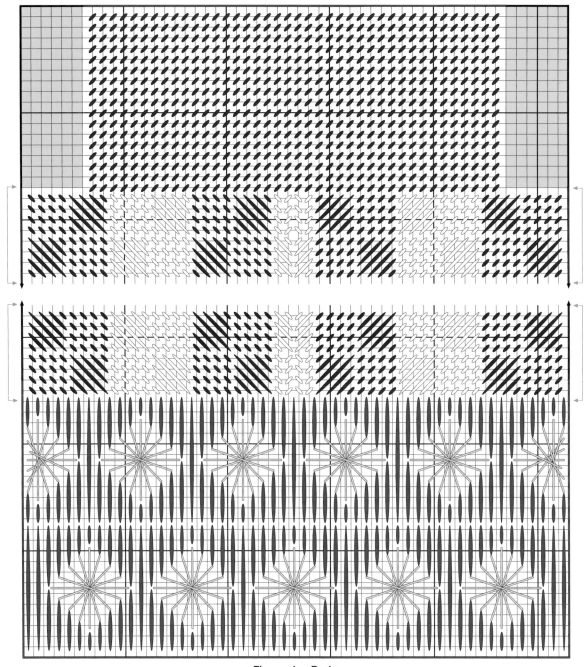

Firecracker Body
53 holes x 150 holes
Cut 2

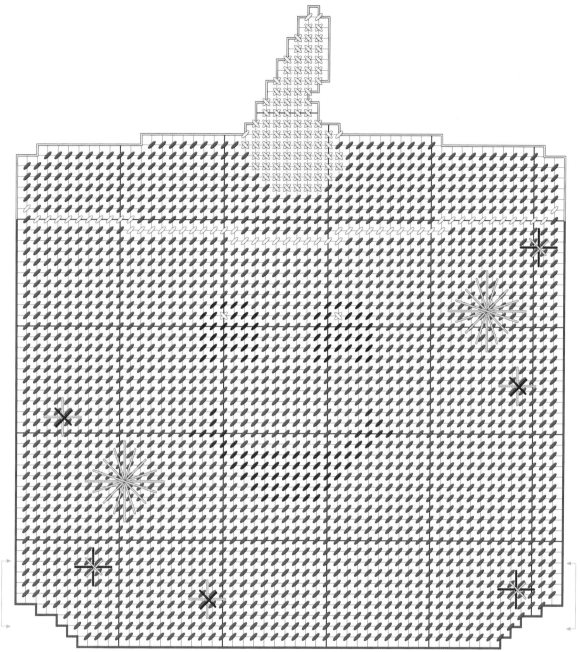

Firecracker Head
53 holes x 60 holes
Cut 2

COLOR KEY

Yards		Medium Weight Yarn
75 (68.6m)	■	Red
55 (50.3m)	■	Royal blue
50 (45.8m)	□	White
5 (4.5m)	□	Yellow
2 (1.9m)	□	Medium blue
1 (1m)	■	Black
1 (1m)	■	Brown
		Uncoded areas on Explosion are yellow Continental Stitches
	✏	Brown Backstitch
		Iridescent Craft Cord
8 (7.4m)	✏	White #55033 Straight Stitch and Diagonal Rhodes Stitch
		Heavy (#32) Braid
3 (2.8m)	✏	Red hi lustre #003HL Straight Stitch

Color numbers given are for Uniek Needloft iridescent craft cord and Kreinik Heavy (#32) Braid.

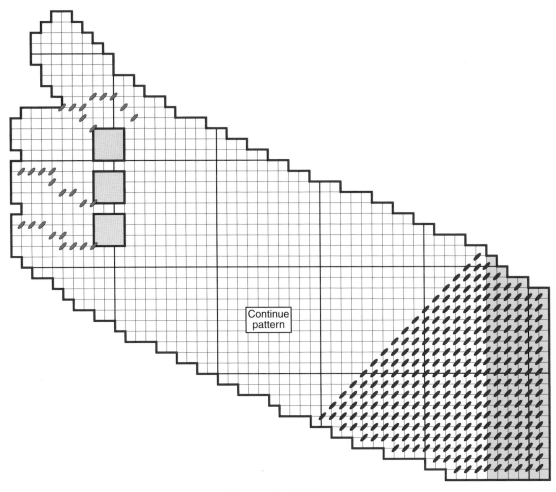

Firecracker Left Arm
52 holes x 44 holes
Cut 2, cutting gray shaded areas from 1 only

COLOR KEY		
Yards	**Medium Weight Yarn**	
75 (68.6m)	■	Red
55 (50.3m)	■	Royal blue
50 (45.8m)	☐	White
5 (4.5m)	☐	Yellow
2 (1.9m)	☐	Medium blue
1 (1m)	■	Black
1 (1m)	■	Brown
		Uncoded areas on Explosion are yellow Continental Stitches
	⁄	Brown Backstitch
	Iridescent Craft Cord	
8 (7.4m)	⁄	White #55033 Straight Stitch and Diagonal Rhodes Stitch
	Heavy (#32) Braid	
3 (2.8m)	⁄	Red hi lustre #003HL Straight Stitch

Color numbers given are for Uniek Needloft iridescent craft cord and Kreinik Heavy (#32) Braid.

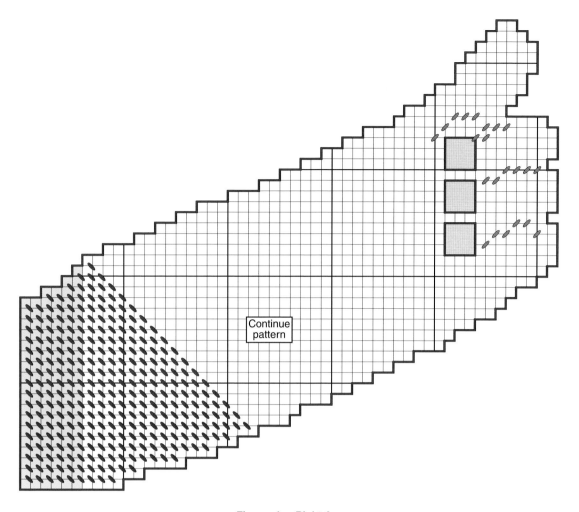

Firecracker Right Arm
52 holes x 44 holes
Cut 2, cutting gray shaded areas from 1 only

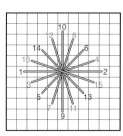

Diagonal Rhodes Stitch

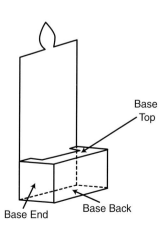

Base Assembly

Ghost & Pumpkin

Size: 12½ inches W x 43 inches H
(31.8cm x 109.2cm)

Skill Level: Intermediate

Materials

❏ Clear 7-count stiff plastic canvas:
   4 (13½ x 22½-inch) sheets
   2 (12 x 18-inch) sheets
❏ Medium weight yarn as listed in color key
❏ Yardstick
❏ Standard-size brick
❏ #16 tapestry needle

Stitching Step by Step

Cutting

1 *Ghost and pumpkin:* Cut two pumpkins, one left hand and one right hand according to graphs. Also cut two upper bodies and two lower bodies, joining graphs for top and bottom portions of each before cutting each in one piece.

2 *Braces:* Cut one piece 44 holes x 9 holes for head brace; one piece 83 holes x 12 holes for upper body brace; one piece 64 holes x 7 holes for lower body brace A; one piece 57 holes x 12 holes for lower body brace B; and one piece 57 holes x 5 holes for lower body brace C.

3 *Base:* Cut one base top and two base front/back pieces according to graphs. Also cut two pieces 17 holes x 51 holes for base ends.

Ghost & Pumpkin

1 *Base:* Stitch base top and *one* front/back piece according to graphs, working Backstitches as you stitch; Overcast edges of base top between red arrows. Using same pattern, stitch both ends. The unstitched piece will be the base front (next to ghost and pumpkin's reverse side).

2 Using orange yarn, Whipstitch base ends to edges of unstitched base front.

3 *Pumpkin:* Holding pieces together, stitch eyes, nose, mouth, rust section lines, stem and outermost orange rows according to graph, working through both layers. Overcast edges.

4 *Ghost:* Holding lower body pieces together, stitch through both layers according to graph, *leaving six rows at bottom unstitched for now as indicated by green shading.*

5 Sandwich the top edge of the unstitched base front between the bottom edges of ghost's lower body. Working through all layers, complete stitching on ghost to join with base front.

6 Holding upper body pieces together and working from top to bottom, begin stitching head. Using black yarn and referring to stitch diagrams (page 24), work Spiderweb Stitch eyes inside blue squares. Finish stitching upper body, including sign, according to graph, leaving the area inside red outlines unstitched. Using black, Backstitch *B* in "Boo" according to graph.

7 *Arms:* Stitch left hand according to graph, Overcasting as you stitch. Wrap black yarn around hand as shown, securing ends on back.

8 Stitch right hand according to graph; Overcast tip between arrows. Position hand on upper body over unstitched area; Whipstitch hand to body according to graph, leaving Overcast tip free and leaving right edge unstitched for now.

9 Align lower and upper bodies edge to edge as shown. Working through all layers, Whipstitch pieces according to graph.

10 Center partially stitched pumpkin on unstitched base front with bottom edges even (it will overlap bottom edge of attached ghost). Working through all layers, finish stitching pumpkin; add orange Backstitches.

11 Using orange yarn and referring to assembly diagram (page 17, for Firecracker) throughout, Whipstitch stitched base back to base ends. Whipstitch base top to base ends and back; Overcast bottom edges.

Braces

Position brace strips across reverse side of ghost where indicated by blue arrows on graphs, in order from top to bottom: head brace, upper body brace, lower body brace A, lower body brace B, lower body brace C. Overcast ghost according to graphs, Whipstitching ends of brace strips as you stitch.

Final Assembly

1 Hot-glue left arm to ghost as shown.

2 Insert brick into base through open bottom. Slide yardstick down back of ghost, through all brace strips and into base.

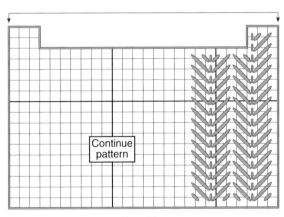

Base Top
26 holes x 17 holes
Cut 1

COLOR KEY

Yards	Medium Weight Yarn
120 (109.8m)	☐ White
75 (68.6m)	▨ Orange
30 (27.5m)	☐ Yellow
25 (22.9m)	■ Black
3 (2.8m)	■ Rust
2 (1.9m)	▨ Dark green
	╱ Black Backstitch and Straight Stitch
	╱ Orange Backstitch

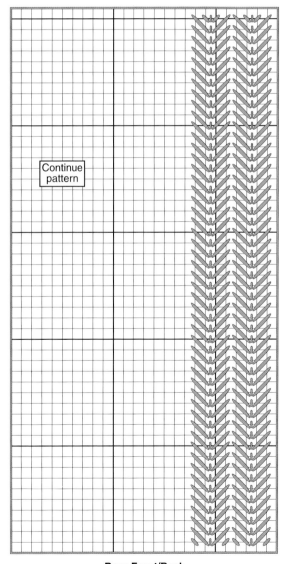

Base Front/Back
26 holes x 51 holes
Cut 2, stitch 1

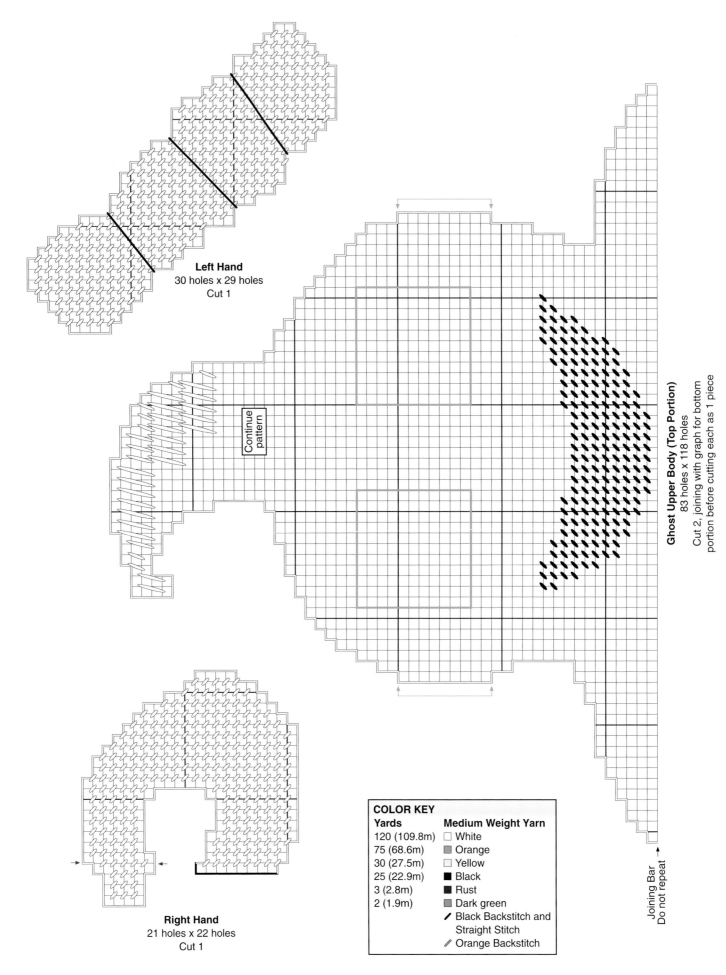

Left Hand
30 holes x 29 holes
Cut 1

Continue pattern

Ghost Upper Body (Top Portion)
83 holes x 118 holes
Cut 2, joining with graph for bottom portion before cutting each as 1 piece

Joining Bar
Do not repeat

Right Hand
21 holes x 22 holes
Cut 1

COLOR KEY

Yards	Medium Weight Yarn
120 (109.8m)	☐ White
75 (68.6m)	▨ Orange
30 (27.5m)	☐ Yellow
25 (22.9m)	■ Black
3 (2.8m)	■ Rust
2 (1.9m)	▨ Dark green
	╱ Black Backstitch and Straight Stitch
	╱ Orange Backstitch

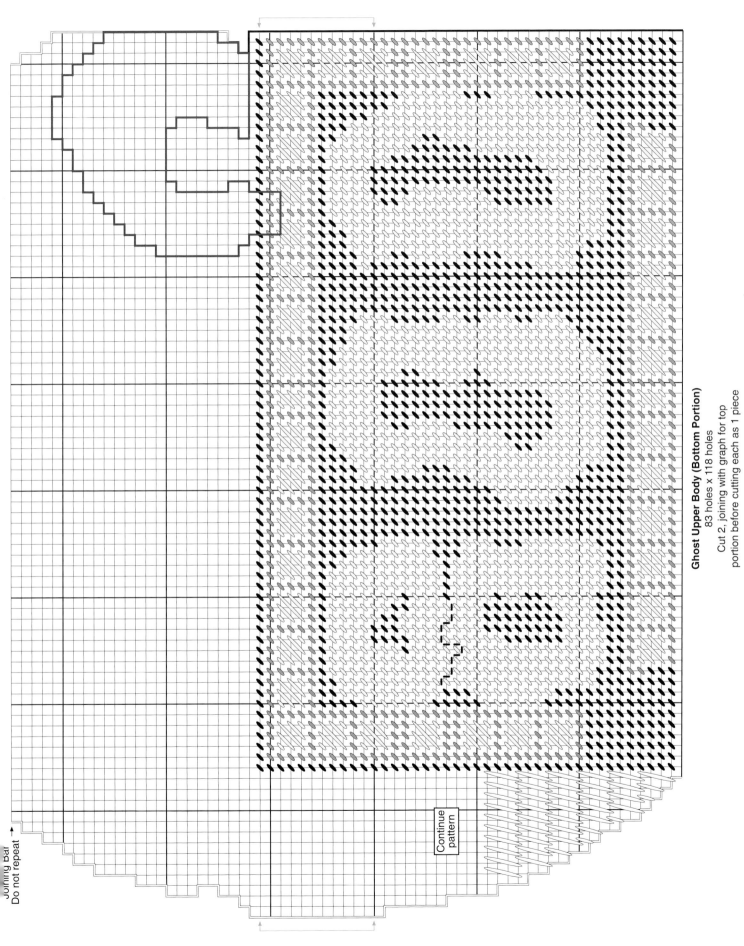

Continue pattern

Ghost Upper Body (Bottom Portion)
83 holes x 118 holes
Cut 2, joining with graph for top
portion before cutting each as 1 piece

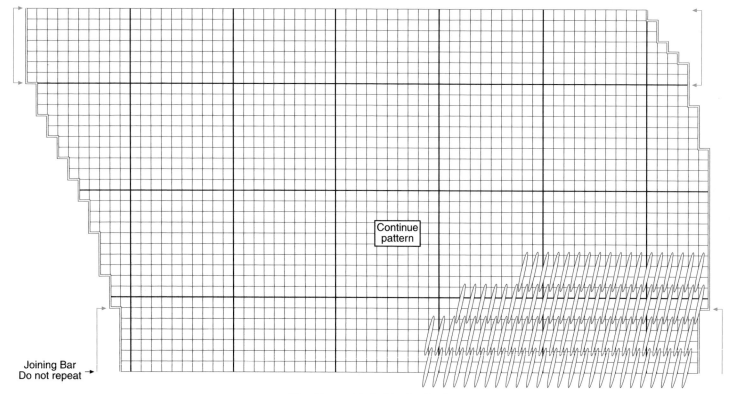

Joining Bar
Do not repeat

Continue
pattern

Ghost Lower Body (Top Portion)
66 holes x 117 holes
Cut 2, joining with graph for bottom
portion before cutting each as 1 piece

COLOR KEY	
Yards	**Medium Weight Yarn**
120 (109.8m)	☐ White
75 (68.6m)	▨ Orange
30 (27.5m)	☐ Yellow
25 (22.9m)	■ Black
3 (2.8m)	■ Rust
2 (1.9m)	▨ Dark green
	╱ Black Backstitch and Straight Stitch
	╱ Orange Backstitch

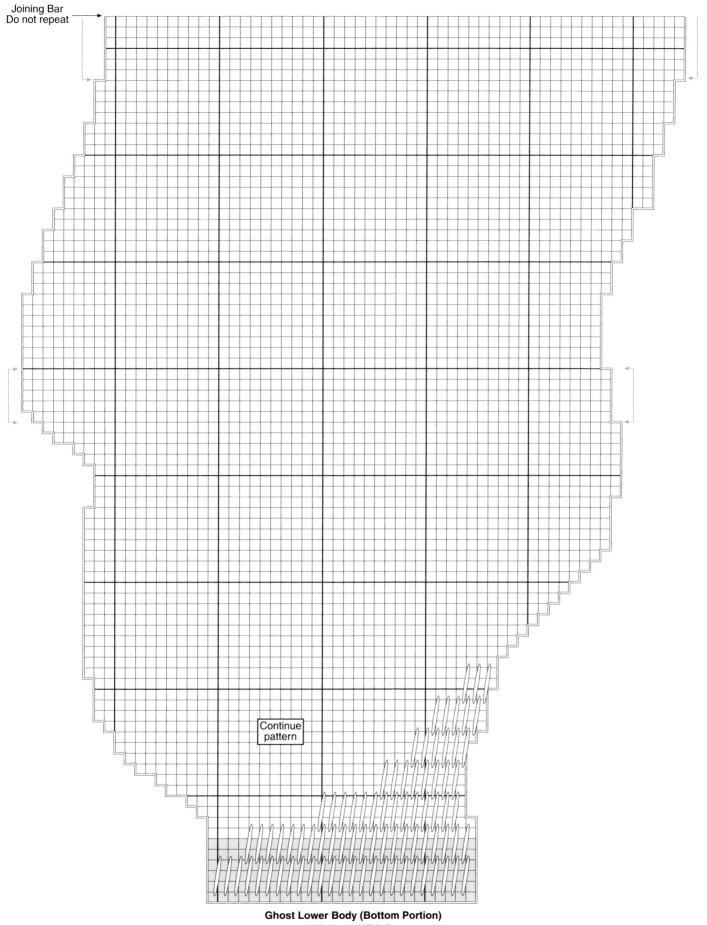

Ghost Lower Body (Bottom Portion)
66 holes x 117 holes
Cut 2, joining with graph for top
portion before cutting each as 1 piece

Continue
pattern

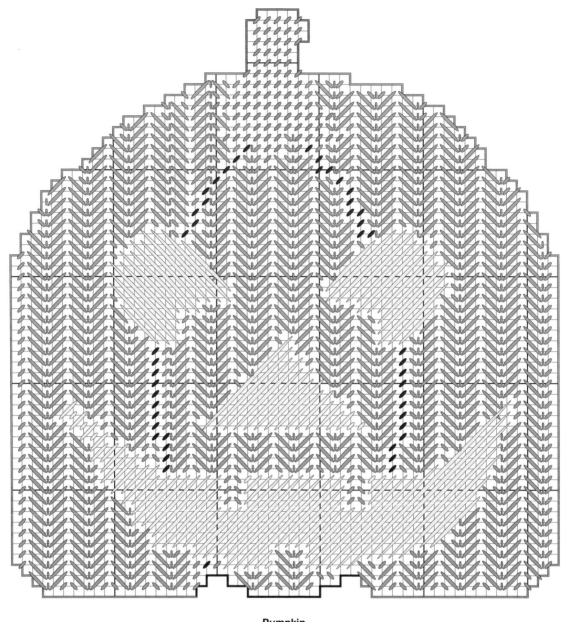

Pumpkin
53 holes x 55 holes
Cut 2

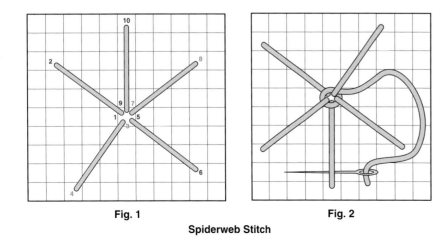

Fig. 1

Fig. 2

Spiderweb Stitch

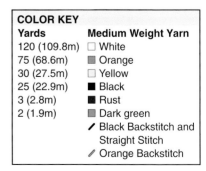

COLOR KEY

Yards	Medium Weight Yarn
120 (109.8m)	☐ White
75 (68.6m)	☐ Orange
30 (27.5m)	☐ Yellow
25 (22.9m)	■ Black
3 (2.8m)	■ Rust
2 (1.9m)	☐ Dark green
✒ Black Backstitch and Straight Stitch
✒ Orange Backstitch

Tom Turkey

Size: 15¼ inches W x 43 inches H
(38.7cm x 109.2cm)
Skill Level: Intermediate

Materials

- ❑ Clear 7-count stiff plastic canvas:
    - 4 (13½ x 22½-inch) sheets
    - 2 (12 x 18-inch) sheets
- ❑ Medium weight yarn as listed in color key
- ❑ Uniek Needloft metallic craft cord as listed in color key
- ❑ 4½ x 40-inch (11.4cm x 101.6cm) piece foam-core board
- ❑ Standard-size brick
- ❑ #16 tapestry needle

Stitching Step by Step

Cutting

1 *Turkey:* Cut one feet piece according to graph. Cut two legs/body pieces, joining graphs for top and bottom portions before cutting each as one piece. Cut two head/tail pieces, joining graphs for left and right portions before cutting each as one piece. Cut one sign according to graph.

2 *Braces and joining strips:* Cut one piece 35 holes x 10 holes for leg brace; one piece 69 holes x 15 holes for body brace; one piece 67 holes x 6 holes for lower sign brace; one piece 66 holes x 6 holes for upper sign brace; one piece 95 holes x 6 holes for tail brace; and one piece 35 holes x 6 holes for feet/legs joining strip.

3 *Base:* Cut one base top and one base back according to graphs. Also cut two pieces 17 holes x 53 holes for base ends.

Turkey

1 Work background stitches on feet piece according to graph, *leaving the last three rows along top edge unstitched for now, as indicated by green shading.*

2 *Body:* Holding legs/body pieces together and working through both layers, stitch according to graph, referring to the stitch diagrams (page 26) to fill in uncoded area at top of legs with light sage Diagonal Cross Stitches, and *leaving three rows along bottom edges unstitched for now as indicated by green shading.* **Note:** *Notice on the stitch diagrams that Diagonal Cross Stitch is worked from lower right to upper left; begin stitching in the lower right corner of areas to be filled with this pattern stitch.*

3 Sandwich edges of feet/legs joining strip between the unstitched rows at bottom of legs/body piece; align bottom half of joining strip behind unstitched rows at top of feet. Stitch through all layers according to graphs to join feet to legs/body.

4 *Base:* Stitch base top and back according to graphs. Overcast edges of base top between red arrows. Using pattern shown on back graph, stitch both ends.

5 Referring to base assembly diagram (for Miss Bunny, page 3) and using light gold yarn through step 6, Whipstitch base back to base ends. Whipstitch base top to base ends and back. *Note: On this design, the base holds the brick vertically.*

6 Center base on reverse side of feet with bottom edges even and side edges of base even with edges of legs. Whipstitch base sides to brown stitches on reverse side of feet and to adjacent edges of legs; Overcast bottom of base.

7 Overcast remainder of feet with dark brown.

8 *Sign:* Stitch sign according to graph, filling in uncoded wings with light sage Diagonal Cross Stitches.

9 Center sign along top edge of legs/body; using light sage yarn, Whipstitch bottom edge of sign to top edge of legs/body.

10 *Head/tail:* Holding head/tail pieces together and working through both layers, stitch according to graph, filling in uncoded head and neck with light sage Diagonal Cross Stitches.

11 Center head/tail along top edge of sign; Whipstitch head/tail to sign using adjacent colors on head/tail.

12 *Work embroidery stitches:* Work Backstitch and Straight Stitch at top of shoes and around buckles using dark brown. Backstitch "happy" on sign using tan. Backstitch between feathers on tail and around head and neck using dark sage. Backstitch around white portion of eyes using black. Straight Stitch buckle on hat using gold metallic craft cord.

13 *Overcast all remaining edges according to graphs, Whipstitching ends of brace strips where indicated by blue arrows on graphs as follows:* Whipstitch leg brace between arrows at top of legs; body brace at upper body; lower sign brace along bottom edge of sign; upper sign brace along top edge of sign; and tail brace along edges of tail feathers.

Final Assembly

Insert brick into base through open bottom. Slide foam core board down back of turkey, through all brace strips, and into base. Tack tail brace to stitching on reverse side as needed with additional stitches to hold foam core board in center.

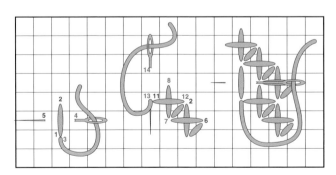

Diagonal Cross Stitch

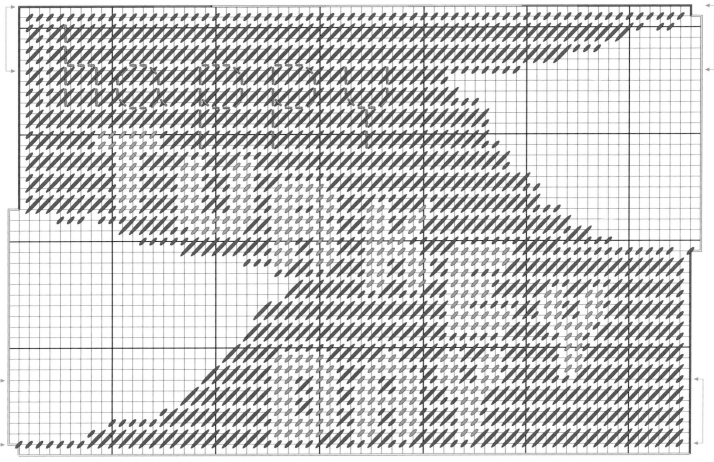

Tom Turkey Sign
67 holes x 42 holes
Cut 1

COLOR KEY	
Yards	**Medium Weight Yarn**
80 (73.2m)	▦ Light gold
52 (47.5m)	▦ Variegated plum/blue/gold/green/red
51 (46.6m)	▦ Dark brown
10 (9.2m)	▦ Dark sage
5 (4.6m)	▦ Dark red
5 (4.6m)	▦ Tan
2 (1.9m)	■ Black
2 (1.9m)	▦ Royal blue
2 (1.9m)	☐ White
51 (46.6m)	Uncoded areas are light sage Diagonal Cross Stitch
	╱ Light sage Overcast and Whipstitch
	╱ Dark brown Backstitch
	╱ Dark sage Backstitch
	╱ Tan Backstitch
	╱ Black Backstitch
	Metallic Craft Cord
5 (4.6m)	☐ Gold #55001
	╱ Gold #55001 Straight Stitch
Color number given is for Uniek Needloft metallic craft cord.	

Tom Turkey Head/Tail (Left Portion)
101 holes x 87 holes
Cut 2, joining with graph for right
portion before cutting each as 1 piece

Joining Bar
Do not repeat

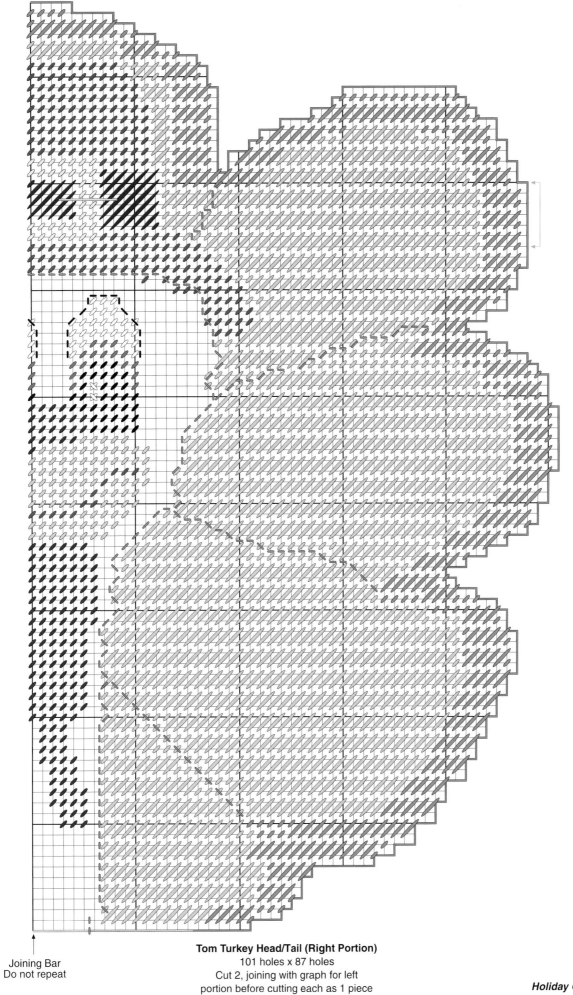

Tom Turkey Head/Tail (Right Portion)
101 holes x 87 holes
Cut 2, joining with graph for left
portion before cutting each as 1 piece

Joining Bar
Do not repeat

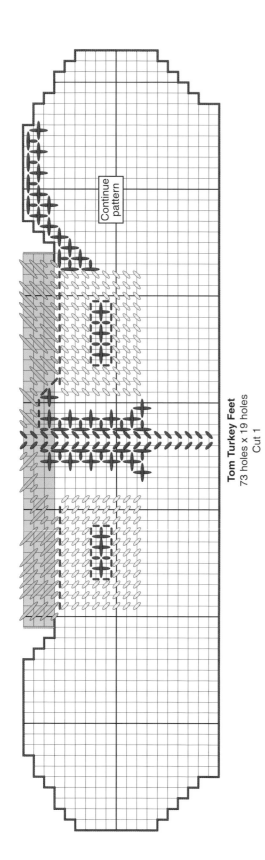

Tom Turkey Feet
73 holes x 19 holes
Cut 1

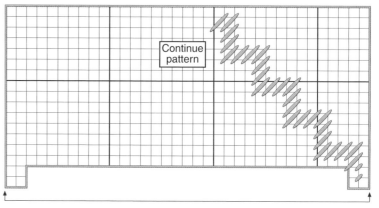

Tom Turkey Base Top
35 holes x 17 holes
Cut 1

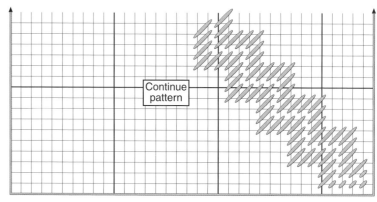

Tom Turkey Base Back
35 holes x 53 holes
Cut 1

COLOR KEY

Yards	Medium Weight Yarn
80 (73.2m)	Light gold
52 (47.5m)	Variegated plum/blue/gold/green/red
51 (46.6m)	Dark brown
10 (9.2m)	Dark sage
5 (4.6m)	Dark red
5 (4.6m)	Tan
2 (1.9m)	Black
2 (1.9m)	Royal blue
2 (1.9m)	White
51 (46.6m)	Uncoded areas are light sage Diagonal Cross Stitch
	Light sage Overcast and Whipstitch
	Dark brown Backstitch
	Dark sage Backstitch
	Tan Backstitch
	Black Backstitch
Metallic Craft Cord	
5 (4.6m)	Gold #55001
	Gold #55001 Straight Stitch

Color number given is for Uniek Needloft metallic craft cord.

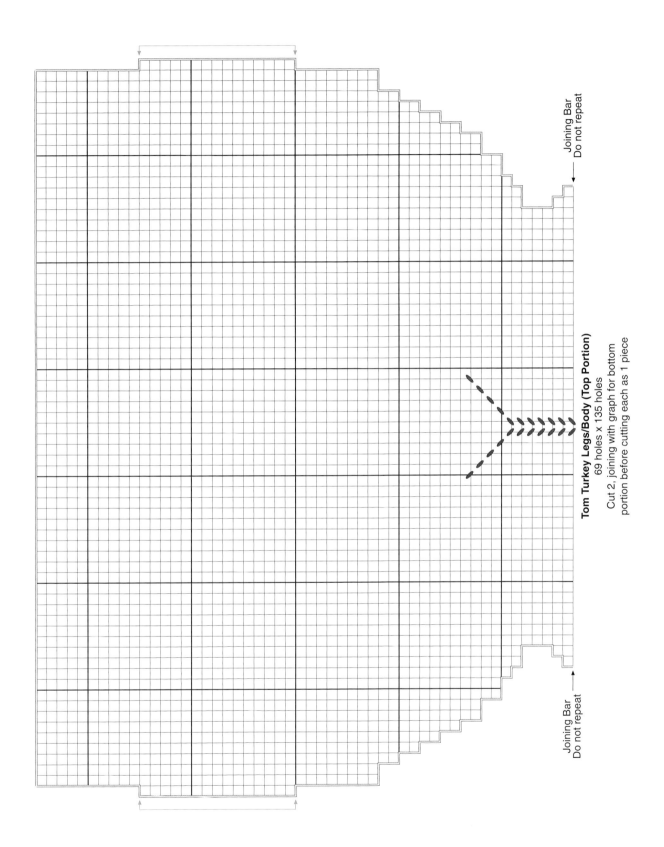

Tom Turkey Legs/Body (Top Portion)
69 holes x 135 holes

Cut 2, joining with graph for bottom
portion before cutting each as 1 piece

Joining Bar
Do not repeat

Joining Bar
Do not repeat

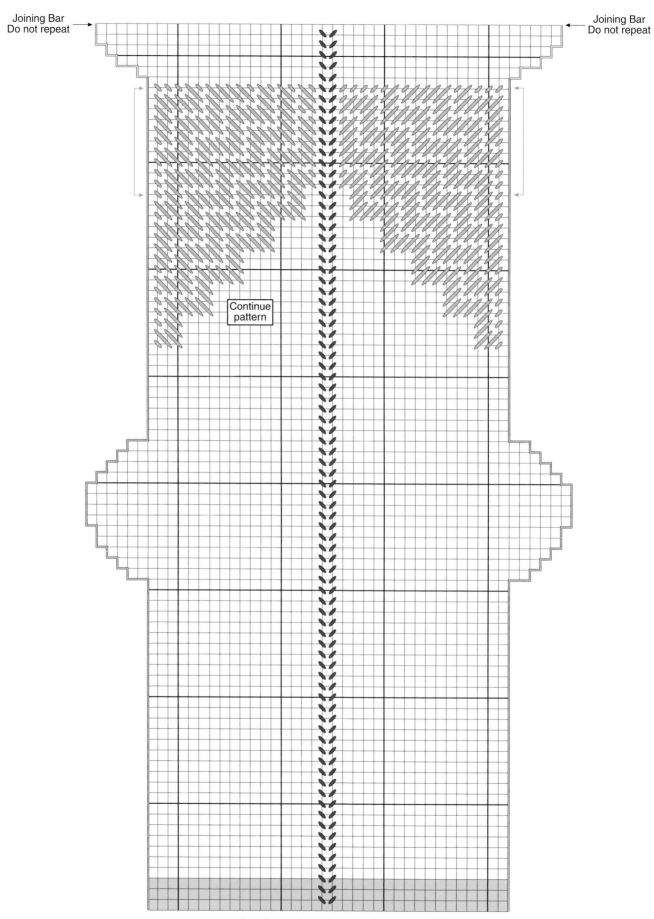

Continue
pattern

Tom Turkey Legs/Body (Bottom Portion)
69 holes x 135 holes
Cut 2, joining with graph for top
portion before cutting each as 1 piece

Santa

Size: 17¾ inches W x 41 inches H
(45.1cm x 104.1cm)

Skill Level: Intermediate

Materials

❑ Clear 7-count stiff plastic canvas:
   3 (13½ x 22½-inch) sheets
   2 (12 x 18-inch) sheets
❑ Medium weight yarn as listed in color key
❑ Uniek Needloft metallic craft cord as listed
   in color key
❑ Yardstick
❑ Standard-size brick
❑ #16 tapestry needle
❑ Hot-glue gun

Stitching Step by Step

Cutting

1 *Santa:* Cut one boots piece, one mustache and two right arms according to graphs. Cut one head, joining graphs for right and left portions before cutting as one piece. Cut two bodies, joining graphs for right and left top and bottom portions before cutting each as one piece. Cut two left sides, joining graphs for top and bottom portions before cutting each as one piece.

2 *Braces and joining strips:* Cut four pieces 12 holes x 6 holes for braces; one piece 81 holes x 12 holes for body/head joining strip; one piece 106 holes x 10 holes for left side joining strip and one piece 81 holes x 6 holes for right side joining strip.

3 *Base:* Cut one base top and two base front/back pieces according to graphs. Also cut two pieces 17 holes x 53 holes for base ends.

Santa & Base

1 *Boots:* Stitch boots according to graph, referring to stitch diagram (page 41) throughout to work off-white Unclipped Turkey Loop Stitches and *leaving area at top above Turkey Loop Stitches unstitched.*

2 *Body:* Holding body pieces together, stitch according to graph, working through both layers and *leaving rows along top, bottom, right and left edges unstitched as indicated by green shading.*

3 Sandwich unstitched rows on boots between unstitched rows at bottom of body. Working through all layers, stitch according to graph to join boots to body.

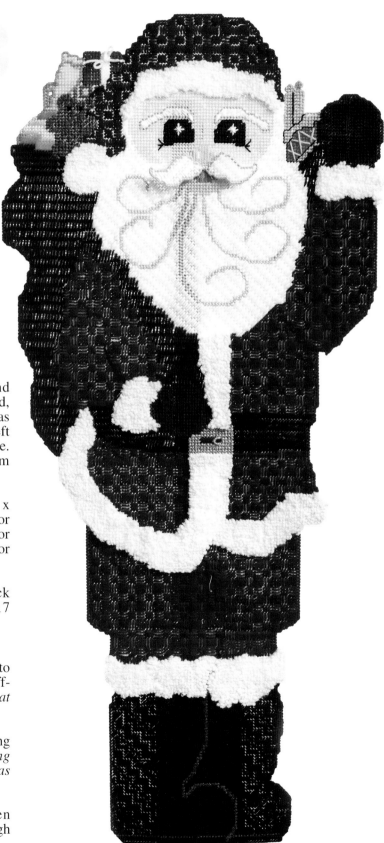

4 *Head:* Stitch head according to graph, *leaving rows along bottom and side edges unstitched where indicated by green shading.*

5 Sandwich bottom six rows on body/head joining strip between unstitched top edges of body, avoiding areas on right and left edges where left side and right arm will be attached. Align top half of joining strip behind bottom edge of head. Working through all layers, stitch over joining strip to join head to body.

6 *Left Side and Right Arm:* Holding pieces together in matching pairs and working through both layers, stitch according to graphs, *leaving rows along side edges unstitched where indicated by green shading.*

7 Sandwich the left side joining strip between the unstitched edges of the left side and the joined head and body, trimming ends of strip as needed to fit. Working through all layers, stitch to join left side to body.

8 In the same manner, join the right arm to the body and head using the right arm joining strip, trimming ends of strip as needed.

9 *Work embroidery stitches:* Using bright red yarn, Straight Stitch teddy bear's mouth. Using black, Straight Stitch Santa's eyes and Backstitch toy adjacent to right arm. Using dark brown, Backstitch sleeves, between legs and tan toy on right side. Using light gray, Backstitch around eyebrows and Straight Stitch toy on right portion of head. Using yellow, Backstitch horn in sack. Using gold metallic cord, work an extended Lazy Daisy Stitch for belt buckle closure according to graph.

10 Stitch mustache according to graph; referring to photo, hot-glue to head.

Base

1 Stitch base top and *one* front/back piece according to graphs; Overcast edges of base top between red arrows. Using same pattern, stitch both ends. The unstitched piece will be the base front (next to Santa's reverse side).

2 Using black yarn throughout, Whipstitch base ends to edges of unstitched base front. Center base front on reverse side of Santa's boots with bottom edges even; stitch edges of base front to Santa, working through stitches on reverse side only.

3 Referring to base assembly diagram (page 3, for Miss Bunny), Whipstitch stitched base back to base ends. Whipstitch base top to base ends and back; Overcast bottom edges.

Braces

1 Center one brace strip on reverse side of Santa in rows indicated by blue arrows on head graph; Whipstitch short ends of brace to head, working under stitches on reverse side only. Repeat to attach remaining brace strips in rows indicated by blue arrows on body graphs.

2 Overcast remaining unfinished edges.

Final Assembly

Insert brick into base through open bottom. Slide yardstick down back of Santa, through all brace strips, and into base.

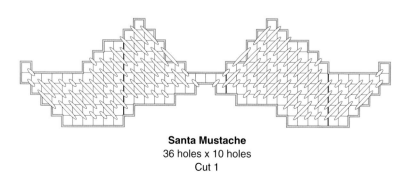

Santa Mustache
36 holes x 10 holes
Cut 1

COLOR KEY	
Yards	**Medium Weight Yarn**
145 (132.6m)	☐ White
55 (50.3m)	■ Dark red
25 (22.9m)	■ Black
15 (13.8m)	■ Dark brown
7 (6.5m)	■ Dark green
4 (3.7m)	☐ Light peach
2 (1.9m)	▨ Bright green
2 (1.9m)	■ Dark gray
2 (1.9m)	▨ Dark royal blue
2 (1.9m)	☐ Light gray
2 (1.9m)	▨ Light pink
1 (1m)	▨ Bright pink
1 (1m)	▨ Bright orange
1 (1m)	■ Dark pink
1 (1m)	☐ Light green
1 (1m)	☐ Peach
1 (1m)	▨ Royal blue
1 (1m)	☐ Tan
1 (1m)	▨ Variegated brown
1 (1m)	☐ Yellow
1 (1m)	▨ Dark gold
1 (1m)	╱ Bright red Straight Stitch
	╱ Black Backstitch and Straight Stitch
	╱ Dark brown Backstitch
	╱ Light gray Backstitch and Straight Stitch
	╱ Yellow Backstitch
	○ Off-white Unclipped Turkey Loop Stitch
	Metallic Craft Cord
2 (1.9m)	☐ Gold #55001
	⊘ Gold #55001 Lazy Daisy Stitch
Color number given is for Uniek Needloft metallic craft cord.	

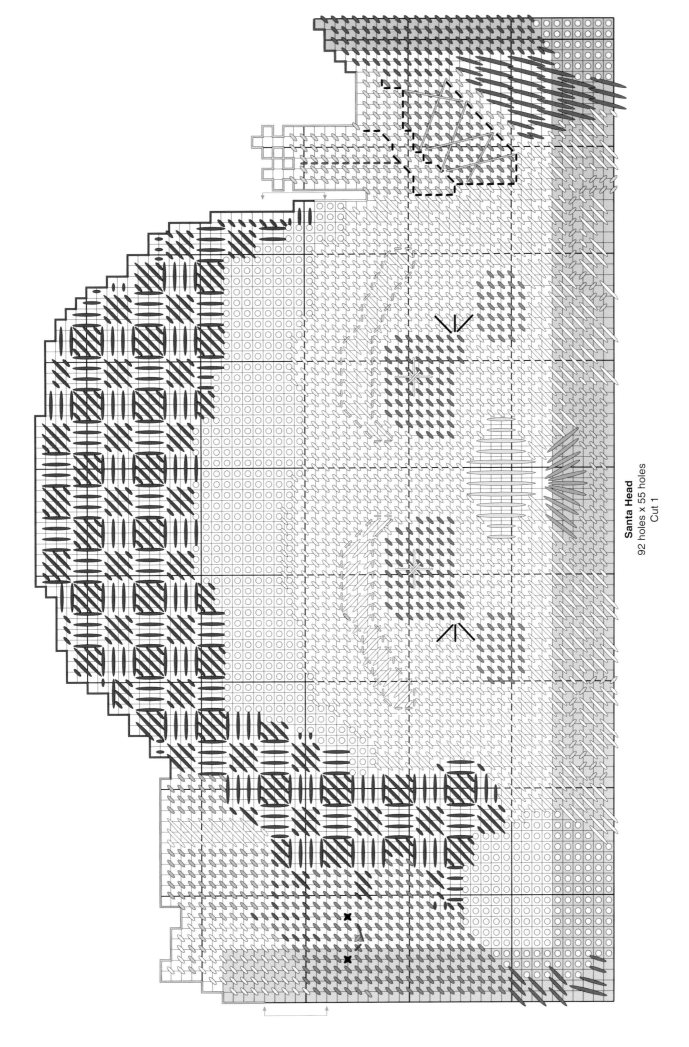

Santa Head
92 holes x 55 holes
Cut 1

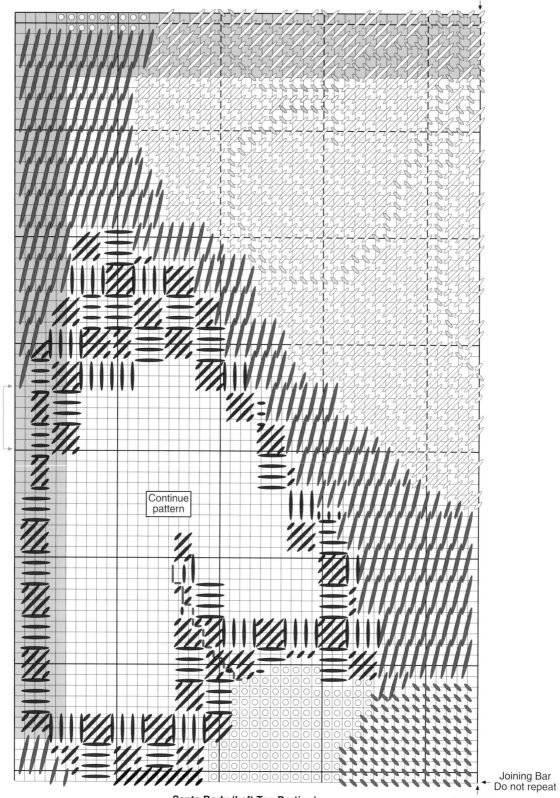

Joining Bar
Do not repeat

Continue
pattern

Joining Bar
Do not repeat

Joining Bar
Do not repeat

Santa Body (Left Top Portion)
91 holes x 150 holes
Cut 2, joining with graphs for left bottom,
right top and right bottom body portions
before cutting each as 1 piece

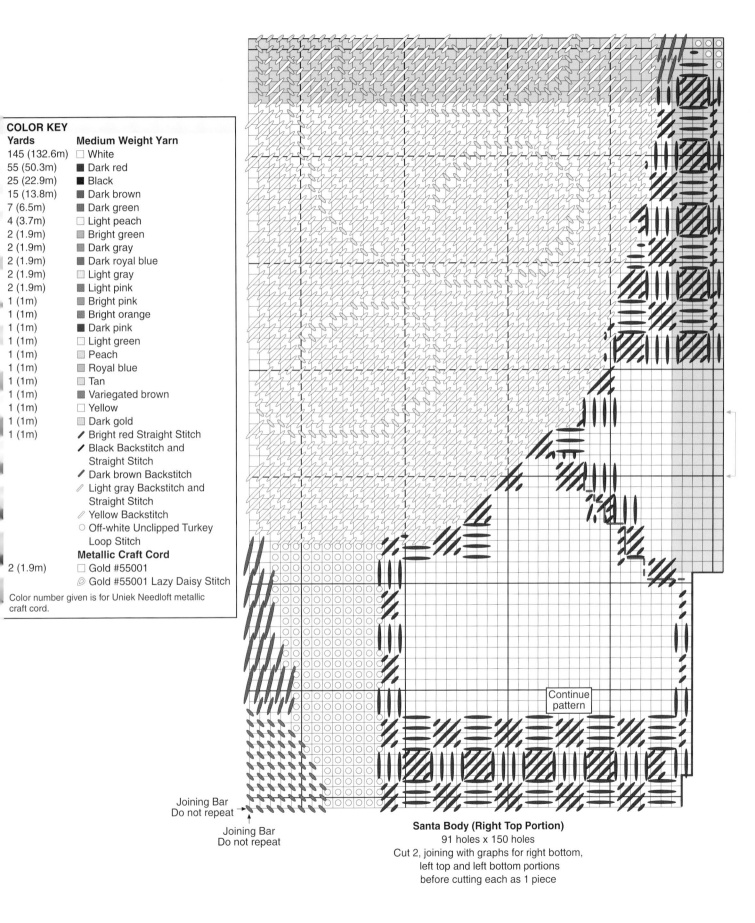

COLOR KEY

Yards	Medium Weight Yarn
145 (132.6m)	☐ White
55 (50.3m)	■ Dark red
25 (22.9m)	■ Black
15 (13.8m)	■ Dark brown
7 (6.5m)	■ Dark green
4 (3.7m)	☐ Light peach
2 (1.9m)	■ Bright green
2 (1.9m)	■ Dark gray
2 (1.9m)	■ Dark royal blue
2 (1.9m)	☐ Light gray
2 (1.9m)	■ Light pink
1 (1m)	■ Bright pink
1 (1m)	■ Bright orange
1 (1m)	■ Dark pink
1 (1m)	☐ Light green
1 (1m)	☐ Peach
1 (1m)	■ Royal blue
1 (1m)	☐ Tan
1 (1m)	■ Variegated brown
1 (1m)	☐ Yellow
1 (1m)	▨ Dark gold
1 (1m)	╱ Bright red Straight Stitch
	╱ Black Backstitch and Straight Stitch
	╱ Dark brown Backstitch
	╱ Light gray Backstitch and Straight Stitch
	╱ Yellow Backstitch
	○ Off-white Unclipped Turkey Loop Stitch
	Metallic Craft Cord
2 (1.9m)	☐ Gold #55001
	◎ Gold #55001 Lazy Daisy Stitch

Color number given is for Uniek Needloft metallic craft cord.

Joining Bar
Do not repeat

Joining Bar
Do not repeat

Continue pattern

Santa Body (Right Top Portion)
91 holes x 150 holes
Cut 2, joining with graphs for right bottom,
left top and left bottom portions
before cutting each as 1 piece

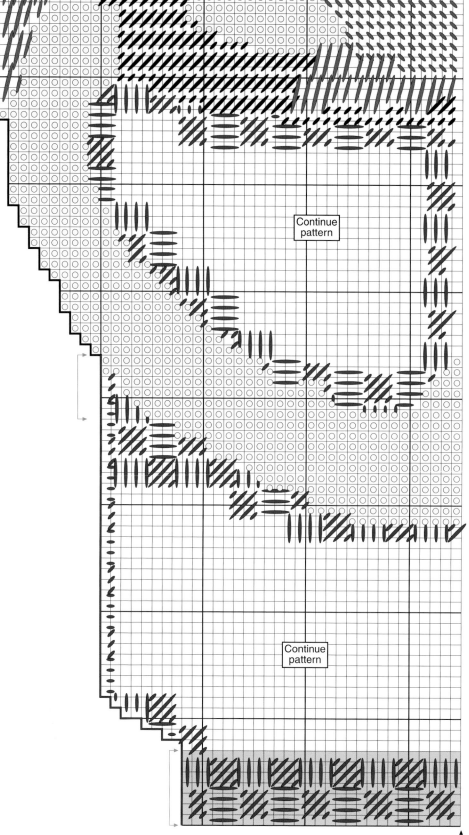

Joining Bar
Do not repeat

Continue
pattern

Continue
pattern

Santa Body (Left Bottom Portion)
91 holes x 150 holes
Cut 2, joining with graphs for left top, right top and right
bottom portions before cutting each as 1 piece

Joining Bar
Do not repeat

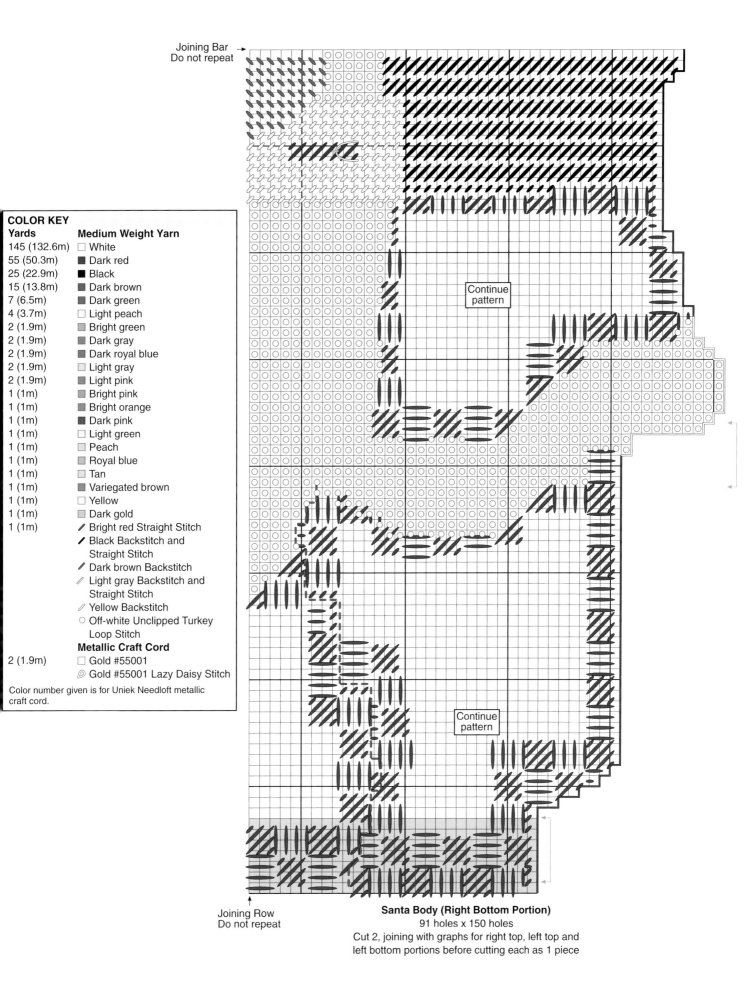

Joining Bar →
Do not repeat

COLOR KEY

Yards	Medium Weight Yarn
145 (132.6m)	☐ White
55 (50.3m)	■ Dark red
25 (22.9m)	■ Black
15 (13.8m)	■ Dark brown
7 (6.5m)	■ Dark green
4 (3.7m)	☐ Light peach
2 (1.9m)	▨ Bright green
2 (1.9m)	■ Dark gray
2 (1.9m)	■ Dark royal blue
2 (1.9m)	☐ Light gray
2 (1.9m)	■ Light pink
1 (1m)	■ Bright pink
1 (1m)	■ Bright orange
1 (1m)	■ Dark pink
1 (1m)	☐ Light green
1 (1m)	☐ Peach
1 (1m)	■ Royal blue
1 (1m)	☐ Tan
1 (1m)	■ Variegated brown
1 (1m)	☐ Yellow
1 (1m)	▨ Dark gold
1 (1m)	╱ Bright red Straight Stitch
	╱ Black Backstitch and Straight Stitch
	╱ Dark brown Backstitch
	╱ Light gray Backstitch and Straight Stitch
	╱ Yellow Backstitch
	○ Off-white Unclipped Turkey Loop Stitch
	Metallic Craft Cord
2 (1.9m)	☐ Gold #55001
	⌀ Gold #55001 Lazy Daisy Stitch

Color number given is for Uniek Needloft metallic craft cord.

Continue pattern

Continue pattern

Joining Row
Do not repeat

Santa Body (Right Bottom Portion)
91 holes x 150 holes
Cut 2, joining with graphs for right top, left top and
left bottom portions before cutting each as 1 piece

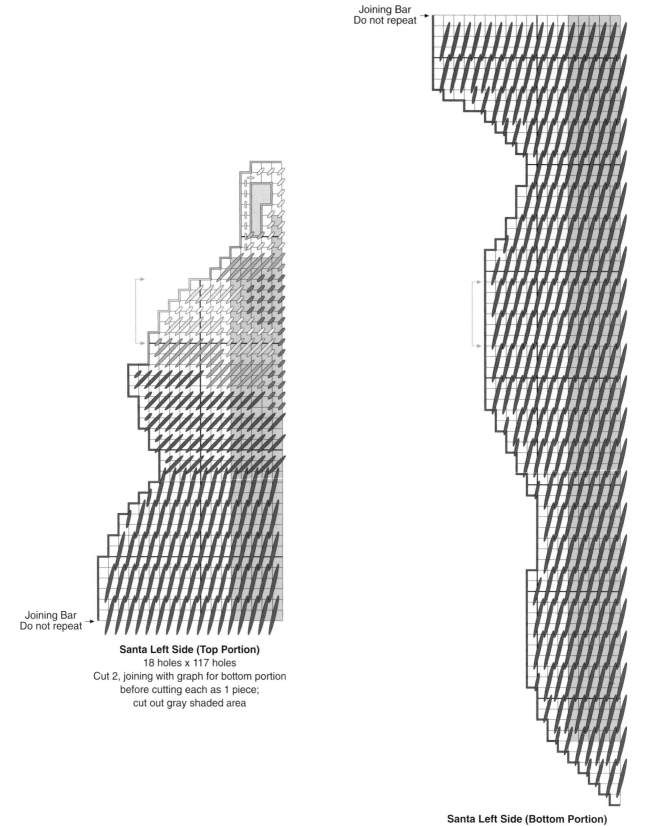

Joining Bar
Do not repeat →

Santa Left Side (Top Portion)
18 holes x 117 holes
Cut 2, joining with graph for bottom portion
before cutting each as 1 piece;
cut out gray shaded area

Joining Bar
Do not repeat →

Santa Left Side (Bottom Portion)
18 holes x 117 holes
Cut 2, joining with graph for top
portion before cutting each as 1 piece

COLOR KEY

Yards	Medium Weight Yarn
145 (132.6m)	☐ White
55 (50.3m)	■ Dark red
25 (22.9m)	■ Black
15 (13.8m)	■ Dark brown
7 (6.5m)	■ Dark green
4 (3.7m)	☐ Light peach
2 (1.9m)	■ Bright green
2 (1.9m)	■ Dark gray
2 (1.9m)	■ Dark royal blue
2 (1.9m)	☐ Light gray
2 (1.9m)	■ Light pink
1 (1m)	■ Bright pink
1 (1m)	■ Bright orange
1 (1m)	■ Dark pink
1 (1m)	☐ Light green
1 (1m)	■ Peach
1 (1m)	■ Royal blue
1 (1m)	☐ Tan
1 (1m)	■ Variegated brown
1 (1m)	☐ Yellow
1 (1m)	▦ Dark gold
1 (1m)	╱ Bright red Straight Stitch
	╱ Black Backstitch and Straight Stitch
	╱ Dark brown Backstitch
	╱ Light gray Backstitch and Straight Stitch
	╱ Yellow Backstitch
	○ Off-white Unclipped Turkey Loop Stitch

Metallic Craft Cord

Yards	
2 (1.9m)	☐ Gold #55001
	⊘ Gold #55001 Lazy Daisy Stitch

Color number given is for Uniek Needloft metallic craft cord.

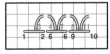

Clipped Turkey Loop

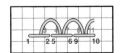

Unclipped Turkey Loop

Right Arm
15 holes x 82 holes
Cut 2

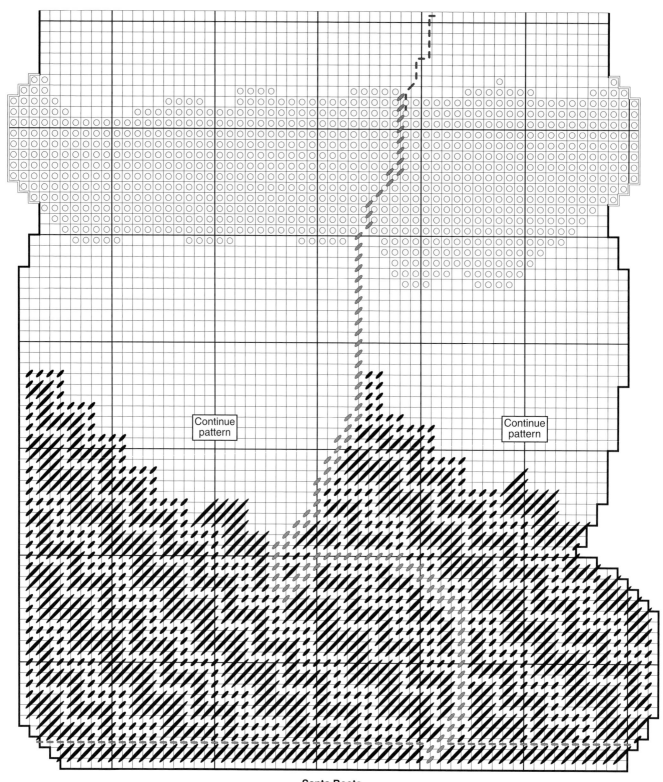

Santa Boots
63 holes x 71 holes
Cut 1

Continue pattern

Continue pattern

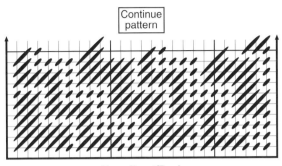

Base Front/Back
26 holes x 53 holes
Cut 2, stitch 1

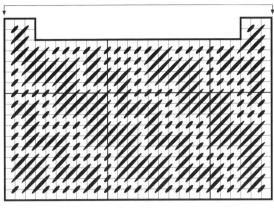

Base Top
26 holes x 17 holes
Cut 1

COLOR KEY	
Yards	**Medium Weight Yarn**
145 (132.6m)	☐ White
55 (50.3m)	■ Dark red
25 (22.9m)	■ Black
15 (13.8m)	▨ Dark brown
7 (6.5m)	▨ Dark green
4 (3.7m)	☐ Light peach
2 (1.9m)	▨ Bright green
2 (1.9m)	▨ Dark gray
2 (1.9m)	■ Dark royal blue
2 (1.9m)	☐ Light gray
2 (1.9m)	▨ Light pink
1 (1m)	▨ Bright pink
1 (1m)	▨ Bright orange
1 (1m)	■ Dark pink
1 (1m)	☐ Light green
1 (1m)	▨ Peach
1 (1m)	▨ Royal blue
1 (1m)	☐ Tan
1 (1m)	▨ Variegated brown
1 (1m)	☐ Yellow
1 (1m)	▨ Dark gold
1 (1m)	✔ Bright red Straight Stitch
	✔ Black Backstitch and Straight Stitch
	✔ Dark brown Backstitch
	⁄ Light gray Backstitch and Straight Stitch
	⁄ Yellow Backstitch
	○ Off-white Unclipped Turkey Loop Stitch
	Metallic Craft Cord
2 (1.9m)	☐ Gold #55001
	◎ Gold #55001 Lazy Daisy Stitch

Color number given is for Uniek Needloft metallic craft cord.

The full line of The Needlecraft Shop
products is carried by Annie's Attic catalog.
TOLL-FREE ORDER LINE
or to request a free catalog
(800) 582-6643
Customer Service
(800) 449-0440
Visit AnniesAttic.com

We have made every effort to ensure the accuracy
and completeness of these instructions. We cannot,
however, be responsible for human error, typographical
mistakes or variations in individual work.

ISBN: 978-1-57367-337-2

Printed in USA

1 2 3 4 5 6 7 8 9

Getting Started

Before You Cut

Buy one brand of canvas for each entire project as brands can differ slightly in the distance between bars. Count holes carefully from the graph before you cut, using the bolder lines that show each 10 holes. These 10-count lines begin from the left side for vertical lines and from the bottom for horizontal lines. Mark canvas before cutting; then remove all marks completely before stitching. If the piece is cut in a rectangular or square shape and is either not worked, or worked with only one color and one type of stitch, the graph is not included in the pattern. Instead, the cutting and stitching instructions are given in the general instructions or with the individual project instructions.

Covering the Canvas

Bring needle up from back of work, leaving a short length of yarn on back of canvas; work over short length to secure. To end a thread, weave needle and thread through the wrong side of your last few stitches; clip. Follow the numbers on the small graphs beside each stitch illustration; bring your needle up from the back of the work on odd numbers and down through the front of the work on even numbers. Work embroidery stitches last, after the canvas has been completely covered by the needlepoint stitches.

Shopping for Supplies

For supplies, first shop your local craft and needlework stores. Some supplies may be found in fabric, hardware and discount stores. If you are unable to find the supplies you need, please call Annie's Attic at (800) 582-6643 to request a free catalog that sells plastic canvas supplies.

Basic Stitches

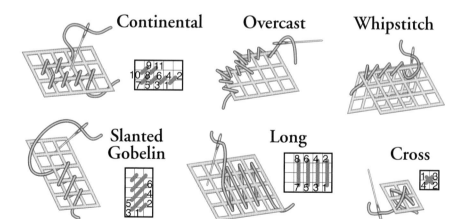

Embroidery Stitches

French Knot  **Lazy Daisy**  **Backstitch**  **Straight**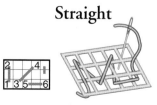

METRIC KEY:
millimeters = (mm)
centimeters = (cm)
meters = (m)
grams = (g)